FAUVE PAINTING 1905-7
THE TRIUMPH OF PURE COLOUR

Published on occasion of the exhibition *Fauve Painting 1905-7:
The Triumph of Pure Colour* at the Courtauld Institute Gallery,
Courtauld Institute of Art, 27 June to 27 August 2001.

Published by the Courtauld Institute Gallery
Designed by Ninety Seven Plus

ISBN 0 904563 16 2

FOREWORD

When Samuel Courtauld began to collect paintings in 1923 he had a clear idea in his mind that the genius of Old Master painting had been re-discovered and revived in the work of those painters who had become known as the Impressionists and Post-Impressionists. By acquiring pictures for the National Gallery, and by founding the collections of the Courtauld Institute Gallery, Courtauld pointed the way to an art for the twentieth century that would be distinctively of the modern world, but yet would be a product of the humane values and creative practices of the western tradition. His view of Modernism was thus open, and ready to accept a wide variety of art in all media, but at least in retrospect it seems clear that, among the movements and counter-movements of European art in the first quarter of the twentieth century, it was among the painters called 'les Fauves' that Courtauld's vision of the future of painting was most aptly realised. Their art, like that of the Impressionists, was based on a mastery of the technical processes of applying paint to canvas, and on a palpable joy in form as it may be perceived through colour. It was also based on the classical tradition of response to nature and to the sense of place, and on an exploratory interest in the sculptural, occasionally monumental presence of the human form in the domestic, rural or urban landscape.

This range of subject matter is fully reflected in the selection of paintings in the present exhibition, fittingly presented in close association with Samuel Courtauld's own collection. The pictures have been assembled from a variety of European sources.

A small group has recently been on loan in Tate Modern, and we are grateful to the Trustees of the Tate Gallery for releasing these paintings now for display in the present exhibition. That loan serves to highlight the importance of the immense contribution of the Fridart Foundation to our understanding of the Fauves, and of other movements within twentieth century Modernism. We are grateful to the Trustees of the Foundation for their generosity in lending to our exhibition.

In particular, however, I should like to thank David and Tanya Josefowitz for their kindness during the planning and preparation of the show, and for their advice on all aspects of presentation. They, together with the group of Courtauld Exhibition Patrons, including Nicholas and Jane Ferguson, Nicholas and Judith Goodison, Henry and Françoise Simon, and the Deborah Loeb Brice Foundation have been essential to our project, and we are deeply grateful for their prompt and enlightened response to the opportunity of showing these paintings in the Gallery. I should also thank my colleagues Ernst Vegelin van Claerbergen, the curator of the exhibition and the author of the accompanying publication, Catherine Putz, the organizer, together with the staff of the Gallery and of Somerset House Arts Fund, for their calm collective efficiency in bringing all to a successful fruition.

JOHN MURDOCH
Director
Courtauld Institute Gallery

FAUVE PAINTING 1905-7
AN INTRODUCTION

Ernst Vegelin van Claerbergen

In June 1905 Henri Matisse sent a postcard to André Derain inviting his young friend to join him at the small southern fishing port of Collioure, where he was spending the summer with his wife and two children: "You would find the most advantageous conditions and your work will reap some benefits here. That's why I repeat again, come.." (Freeman 1995, p. 200). Derain accepted the invitation and arrived in Collioure on July 8th. Matisse had been impressed by the bold work that Derain and Maurice de Vlaminck had been producing in the suburbs of Paris at Chatou, where the two friends shared a studio, and he had helped persuade Derain's parents to support their son's chosen career. Now, working side by side, responding to the strong light and colours of the south, sharing ideas and seeking to advance their previous investigations, the two artists embarked on a period of intense activity and innovation. By the end of the summer Matisse had produced approximately forty watercolours, one hundred drawings and fifteen oils. Derain returned to Paris with some thirty canvases, twenty drawings and fifty sketches. Characterised by the unrestrained use of pure colour, exuberant brushwork and an overwhelming sense of energy, the paintings produced at Collioure in the summer of 1905 have come to embody what we think of as Fauvism. Their bold and experimental nature represented, in Derain's words, "a renewal of expression" (Paris 1999-2000, p. 428).

"The walls were covered with canvases – presenting what seemed to me then a riot of color – sharp and startling, drawing crude and uneven, distortions and exaggerations – composition primitive as though done by a child...It seemed to me grotesque. We asked ourselves, are these things to be taken seriously?" (Freeman 1990, p. 82). *Claribel Cone, recalling room 7 of the 1905 Salon d'Automne*

The Parisian public was first exposed to the new works, the 'lab experiments' as one critic called them, at the Salon d'Automne of 1905. Paintings submitted by André Derain, Henri Matisse and Maurice de Vlaminck were grouped in room 7 with works by three artists who, like Matisse, had trained in the studio of Gustave Moreau at the École des Beaux-Arts: Henri Manguin, Albert Marquet and Charles Camoin. Although Matisse observed that the work of his old friends, who had also spent the summer in the south, was "rather the opposite of mine" (Freeman 1990, p. 79) there were enough similarities for critics and members of the public to respond to the works as a group. Observing the incongruous juxtaposition of the brightly coloured and loosely executed paintings with a classically modelled marble bust, Louis Vauxcelles, a critic for the daily *Gil Blas*, noted wryly that it was a case of "Donatello among the wild beasts [fauves]" (Paris 1999-2000, p. 415). By 1906 the term 'wild beasts' had taken hold and was also being applied to the three painters from Le Havre – Othon Friesz, Raoul Dufy and Georges Braque – who complete what is now understood as the core Fauve group.

In view of the somewhat chaotic account of contemporary art presented in the Salons and commercial galleries of Paris, it is not surprising that critics should have attempted to isolate and label groups of painters such as the Fauves. However, to the painters themselves the term 'Fauve' had little meaning other than perhaps conveying a sense of their brash youthful vigour. Rather than a coherent and well-defined group, the Fauves are better understood as a collection of more or less like-minded friends. They never fully embraced the means of promoting the group identity created for them by critics and the market. There were no exclusive Fauve exhibitions and unlike other avant-garde manifestations, such as the almost contemporaneous *Die Brücke* group in Germany, the Fauves never produced a manifesto. The degree of stylistic convergence implied by the label was also largely absent from Fauve painting.

Although Louis Vauxcelles was moderately supportive of the group that he named, others were less kind. It was the style of the paintings in room 7 rather than their generally trouble-free subject matter that disturbed most critics. The opinion expressed by Marcel Nicolle in the *Journal de Rouen* may be considered typical of the more conservative commentators: "Aside from the materials used, that which we are presented with does not have any connection with painting; presenting some odd medleys of colour; of blue, of red, of yellow, of green; touches of crude colourings juxtaposed haphazardly; barbaric and naive games of a child playing with a 'colouring box'" (Paris 1999-2000, p. 415; Freeman 1990, p. 81). The paintings seemed to reject the conventional criteria of technical skill and representational accuracy by which art was still often judged. The loose and expressive application of paint appeared crude and unfinished. The draughtsmanship was judged incompetent and the compositions clumsy. The colours bore no relation to that which was depicted and their piercing juxtaposition was thought to be unrefined and deliberately shocking. The painters exhibiting in room 7 of the Salon d'Automne did have some support but even those who defended their right to show experimental work and were able to sense the advent of a significant new artistic development had difficulty reconciling themselves with the more daring aspects of Fauve painting.

Matisse would later recall the dual sense of anxiety and opportunity experienced by the painter searching for a distinctive voice in turn-of-the-century Paris, "The artist, encumbered with all the techniques of the past and present, asked himself: 'What do I want?' This was the dominating anxiety of Fauvism"(Freeman 1995, p. 13). That the answer proposed by the Fauves should be framed largely in terms of colour is not entirely surprising. The Fauves were deeply engaged with the work of their predecessors and contemporaries. They trained and reached their maturity in an artistic milieu where colour was a growing preoccupation.

The art world in Paris around 1900 presented an unprecedented range of modernising styles and theoretical persuasions. Of the older generation Claude Monet, Pierre-Auguste Renoir and Edgar Degas were still productive and Impressionism, broadly defined, remained both very much alive and contentious. Retrospective exhibitions at the Salon des Indépendants and the Salon d'Automne, and shows in commercial galleries, ensured that the work of the chief Post-Impressionists was becoming widely accessible. The tremors generated by Paul Cézanne in Provence were starting to be felt, and the work of Paul Gauguin (d.1903), Vincent van Gogh (d.1890) and Georges Seurat (d.1891) was already exercising a considerable influence on the new generation. Gauguin's paintings could be seen in Ambroise Vollard's gallery in 1903 and 1904. Van Gogh was exhibited by Bernheim-Jeune in 1901. Paul Signac and the Neo-Impressionists had developed Seurat's divisionism into a powerful force which dominated the Salon des Indépendants and enjoyed high visibility in the commercial galleries. Pierre Bonnard, Édouard Vuillard and the Nabis circle presented another well-defined and theoretically coherent group. Symbolism was gradually losing its vitality but the work of selected masters, such as the luminous pastels of Odilon Redon, was still held in high esteem.

The increasing use of non-naturalistic colour was very much a feature of this landscape and it was certainly not restricted to artists working in established groups or as part of clearly defined stylistic genealogies. Colour had become a major preoccupation of young artists seeking to assimilate and advance the achievements of their nineteenth century precursors. Forward-looking critics such as Roger Marx commented on this and the term *coloristes* was also being used in commercial circles. The paintings which Louis Valtat (1869-1952) produced in the mid-1890s at Arcachon on the south-west coast of France are often cited as an example of the increasingly liberated use of colour. Similarly non-naturalistic qualities are found in the work of the now somewhat forgotten René Seyssaud (1867-1952). The artists who became the Fauves were very much part of this general development. Although Albert Marquet's claim that he was painting in a Fauve manner by 1898 remains largely unsubstantiated, Matisse's work at this time does show a heightened colour sense. The early stirrings within the Fauve group were not just limited to the alumni of Gustave Moreau's studio. The van Gogh exhibition at Galerie Bernheim-Jeune in 1901 powerfully influenced Vlaminck's expressive and daring use of unmixed colours. Visiting Derain and Vlaminck in Chatou early in 1905, a startled Matisse recorded that, "Vlaminck insisted on absolutely pure colours, on a vermilion that was absolutely vermilion" (Freeman 1990, p. 66). At this time Matisse was preparing his Neo-Impressionist *Luxe, calme et volupté* for the Salon des Indépendants. This celebrated canvas was acquired by Paul Signac whose influential text *D'Eugène Delacroix au néo-impressionisme* (1899) had given the pursuit of colour such compelling historical momentum.

Although it is possible to describe the early development of the Fauve painters, particularly the origins of their liberated use of colour, in terms of their nineteenth century predecessors and established contemporaries such as Signac, to present Fauve painting simply as assimilation and creative synthesis would be to underestimate the extent to which it was radically and deliberately new. Matisse's question, 'What do we want' was not just a matter of selecting and adapting existing styles, it was experienced as an urge for a new mode of expression, one that would reject the perceived refinement of Impressionism and articulate the vigor and optimism of the new century. In a work such as Matisse's *The Red Beach* (no. 1), painted at Collioure in the summer of 1905, colour has fully escaped the confines of naturalistic representation. Matisse has moved beyond the interest in heightened local hues characteristic of his early study of Impressionism and has broken with the methodical colour system advocated by Signac. The beach is a rich red, the headland bright yellow and the sea an arbitrary pattern of blue, green and pink over broadly exposed areas of white canvas. The varied and rapid brushwork, the simplification of forms, the insistent flatness of the design all support the use of colour as an instinctive, emotionally-charged and highly individualistic means of self-expression.

For both Matisse and Derain the summer of 1905 was a turning point. Although surviving correspondence indicates that their achievements involved considerable effort, at Collioure they developed the confidence and the technical means to pursue an artistic practice based on the individual's direct and spontaneous response to the visible world. Their uninhibited use of pure colour and expressive brushwork galvanised the other Fauves. Painting in Chatou, Vlaminck had already proceeded some distance down the path which Albert Marquet, Henri Manguin and Charles Camoin now also followed, albeit somewhat more cautiously. Raoul Dufy, Othon Friesz and the young Georges Braque

would soon also be feeling their way forward, away from a practice
still based on the transcription of nature towards a more instinctive
and personal vision.

The paintings produced at Collioure in the summer of 1905 describe
the thrilling discovery of paint liberated from the conventional
requirements of representation. However, the experimental nature of
this work, the urgency and restlessness which had been fundamental
to the emergence of Fauvism, did not now give way to a period of
consolidation. Both Matisse and Derain were soon seeking to refine and
develop what they had learned. One may speculate that the expressive
violence of works such as *The Red Beach* was antithetical to Matisse's
almost instinctive desire to create an art of balance and harmony. It was
perhaps Derain who gave fullest expression to the discoveries made at
Collioure, but he too was soon looking ahead. Writing to Matisse from
L'Estaque in 1906 he noted with characteristic self-awareness, "I sense
that I am orienting myself toward something better" (Freeman 1990,
p. 92). Both artists would conceive of this reorientation largely in terms
of drawing and a renewed sense of design. Derain and Matisse gradually
abandoned the mixed technique which they had used at Collioure in
favour of more ambitious compositions featuring clearly defined areas
of smooth flat colour. The direct experience of nature which had fed
the frenetic energy of their early work was now increasingly replaced
by subjects drawn from the imagination. Derain's *The Dance* (no. 4)
is an outstanding example of this new Fauve style.

The other Fauves did not follow the new direction proposed by Matisse and Derain. Vlaminck continued to paint in his signature style, applying high-key colours in heavy impasto. Camoin's work remained comparatively restrained and naturalistic. Marquet's palette became more subdued after the initial excitement of his exposure to the Collioure works and Manguin did not substantially alter the luminous manner which he had developed in his idyllic southern pictures of 1905 (no. 8). Braque's *Port of L'Estaque* (no. 13), painted in 1906, and Friesz's *Landscape at La Ciotat* (no. 10), illustrate that the artists from Le Havre, relative latecomers to Fauvism, were finding their distinctive voices just as Matisse and Derain were decisively shifting course. It is Cézanne who is conventionally invoked to explain the developments which now brought the short-lived Fauve movement to a close.

Although the impact of Cézanne can be overstated in relation to the internal momentum of Fauvism, it is indisputable that Cézanne's death in 1906 produced a surge of interest in his work. This was fueled by retrospectives at the Salon des Indépendants and the Salon d'Automne in 1907. Brilliant pure colour began to drain out of Fauve painting and was replaced by a renewed interest in volume and form. Raoul Dufy's 1907 *Boats at Martigues* (no. 12) is characteristic of these developments, demonstrating a deliberate structural treatment of form entirely at odds with the spontaneous expressive spirit of Fauve painting as it had been defined at Collioure in 1905. Derain and Matisse developed similar interests but it was Braque, the youngest of the Fauves and the last to join the core group, who would pursue these tendencies most systematically and, together with Pablo Picasso, create a radically new formal language that would soon eclipse pure colour as the chief concern of the avant-garde. Reviewing an exhibition of 27 works by Braque at Galerie Kahnweiler, Louis Vauxcelles, originator of the Fauve label, noted that Braque was "reducing everything, site and figures and houses, to some geometric schemes, to cubes" (Freeman 1990, p. 113).

Although a variant of the high-key colour painting initiated by the Fauves continued to be practised for years after 1907, and the term itself remained current, the historical phenomenon which was first registered at the Salon d'Automne of 1905 had passed. In fact Fauvism was so short-lived, the pace of change so rapid and the artistic personalities of its chief practitioners so distinct that its characterisation as a movement must be regarded as problematic. Derain described the Fauve years as an "ordeal by fire", as if they were Modernism's right of passage (Paris 1999-2000, p.11). However inherently individualistic and fragmented it may have been, Fauvism certainly gave a decisive impulse to the renewal of painting at the beginning of the twentieth century. That it did so in terms of self-expression and by means of the visually stunning use of pure colour may explain its continued appeal and power.

I

HENRI MATISSE (1869-1954)
La Plage Rouge, 1905
(The Red Beach)

Provenance
Pierre Matisse Gallery, New York; Wright Ludington, Santa Barbara;
Fridart Foundation.

Henri Matisse trained for a career in the law and initially worked as clerk in Saint-Quentin in northern France. Having taken up painting during a long convalescence, he enrolled in the Académie Julian in Paris in 1891. Dissatisfied with his instruction he started attending Gustave Moreau's classes in 1892 and won an official place at the École des Beaux-Arts in 1895. In Moreau's studio Matisse painted with Albert Marquet, Henri Manguin and later with Charles Camoin. He met André Derain in 1899 and was introduced by him to Maurice de Vlaminck at the van Gogh exhibition held by Galerie Bernheim-Jeune in 1901. Matisse spent the summer of 1904 in Saint-Tropez with the leading Neo-Impressionist painter and theorist Paul Signac, an experience which gave rise to his major divisionist canvas *Luxe, calme et volupté*. The following summer was spent with André Derain at Collioure and has come to be regarded as seminal in the history of Fauve painting.

This view of Collioure, a small fishing port near the French border with Spain, is typical of the experimental work which Matisse produced in the summer of 1905. Matisse has moved beyond the systematic divisionist methods practised by the Neo-Impressionists in favour of a direct and instinctive technique which expresses his spontaneous subjective response to the scene. Large areas of the canvas have been left bare and the overall appearance is that of a rapidly executed sketch. Paint has been applied in a highly expressive variety of brushstrokes, ranging from small rectangular strokes to larger passages of dense colour. The colours themselves are fully independent of any descriptive function. Undiluted greens, pinks, reds, yellows and blues create a brilliant pattern which forcefully rejects conventional pictorial representation.

La Plage Rouge was included in Matisse's exhibition at Galerie Druet in 1906 and in the exhibition organised by the Cercle de l'Art Moderne in Le Havre later that same year. By this time Matisse was developing a more graceful linear Fauve style characterised by the use of flat areas of unmodulated colour.

2

HENRI MATISSE (1869-1954)
Femme au Kimono, c.1906
(Woman in a Kimono)

Provenance
Galerie Druet, Paris; Michael Stein, Paris (and Palo Alto, California);
Private collection.

The model for this picture was Matisse's wife Amélie, recognisable by her arching eyebrows and distinctive high cheekbones. Matisse frequently used his wife as a model and painted her in Japanese robes on several occasions. André Derain, Charles Camoin and Albert Marquet also all painted Amélie Matisse in Japanese dress. This work shows Amélie in an informal pose with her hands crossed in her lap. She is seated next to a table on which fruit and a vase of flowers can be made out. The blue background has been interpreted as a view through an open window with the area of pale lilac and red possibly indicating a shutter. Matisse has avoided drawing the outline of the figure, instead brushing in patches of colour to suggest the patterning and decorative effect of the kimono. As a characteristic feature of Japanese art, the flat two-dimensional quality of this work seems particularly appropriate to its subject matter.

The first owners of *Femme au Kimono* were Michael and Sarah Stein, who became close friends of Matisse after meeting him in late 1905. *Femme au Kimono* was displayed in their apartment at 58 rue Madame in Paris. The Stein family provided valuable early support for Matisse and were among the most important collectors of his work. Leo and Gertrude Stein, Michael's brother and sister, acquired Matisse's highly controversial *Woman with a Hat* from the 1905 Salon d'Automne. Sarah was instrumental in the establishment of Matisse's academy which opened in January 1908 in the disused convent (the Couvent des Oiseaux) where Matisse had been renting a studio.

Henri Matisse

3

ANDRÉ DERAIN (1880–1954)
La Tamise et Tower Bridge, 1906
(The Thames and Tower Bridge)

Provenance

Ambroise Vollard, Paris; Etienne Bignou, Paris; Alex Reid & Lefevre, London;
David Eccles, London; Emil-Georg Bührle, Zurich; Dr. Fritz Nathan, Zurich;
John MacAulay, Toronto; Alex Reid & Lefevre, London; Fridart Foundation.

André Derain was born in Chatou in the suburbs of Paris. In 1898 he enrolled in the Académie Camillo where he studied with Eugène Carrière and met both Henri Matisse and Albert Marquet. His close friendship with Maurice de Vlaminck started in 1900. The two artists shared a studio on the Île de Chatou and painted together along the banks of the Seine. Derain rejoined Vlaminck after completing his three-year military service in 1904. Although the works which he and Vlaminck produced in Chatou and the neighbouring towns demonstrate an increasingly bold and liberated sense of colour, Derain's Fauve style emerged fully in the summer of 1905, which he spent with Matisse in Collioure. He wrote to Vlaminck that "All that I have made up until now seems foolish to me" (Freeman 1995, p. 74). Derain exhibited nine paintings at the Salon d'Automne of 1905.

In January 1906 Derain travelled to London to produce a series of paintings for the dealer Ambroise Vollard (who had already purchased the entire contents of his studio). This enterprise was directly motivated by the example of Claude Monet whose views of the Thames had met with considerable critical and commercial success when they were shown at Galerie Durand-Ruel in May-June 1904. Like Monet, Derain was principally drawn to the Thames, painting the Houses of Parliament, various bridges and the commercial life of what was then still a major port. Six of the thirty surviving views include Tower Bridge. This example shows the blue silhouette of the popular tourist attraction with commercial shipping in the Pool of London. The picture also describes the technical variety which characterises Derain's London pictures, combining areas of brushed paint in the sky with flat unmodulated colour in the boats at the lower corners and single strokes in parts of the river. Derain wrote to Vlaminck from London that he was "working like a horse" (Freeman 1995, p. 88) but he also took the opportunity to visit museums, admiring the work of, among others, J.M.W. Turner at the National Gallery.

4

ANDRÉ DERAIN (1880-1954)
La Danse, c.1906
(The Dance)

Provenance

Léon Pédron, Paris; Hôtel Drouot, Paris (2 June 1927, lot 12, as Fresque Hindou); M. Renould, Paris;
Knoedler & Co., New York; Parke-Bernet, New York (14 October 1965, lot. 131); Pedro Vallenilla Echeverria, Caracas;
Galerie Marcel Bernheim, Paris; Fridart Foundation.

La Danse is one of the most ambitious and enigmatic of all Derain's Fauve paintings. Three highly stylised figures, apparently female, are arranged in frieze-like fashion in a shallow and schematically rendered landscape. A snake winds its way between them. The woman to the left supports a magnificently plumed bird on her right hand. The striated pattern of her dress, which recalls Byzantine painting, is repeated in the trees. The figure at the right, seen from behind, has turned her head towards the central action. A fourth figure is seated in the background. Despite the crude drawing, evident particularly in the hands and feet, the arrangement of the figures generates a graceful flowing line through the composition. The colour scheme is dominated by dark orange, blue and green, with the flat yellow providing a powerfully abstract backdrop to the stage-like setting.

La Danse illustrates the remarkable changes that Derain's painting had undergone since the summer of 1905. The explosive mixed brushwork employed with such conviction at Collioure has been replaced by large areas of flat colour and a concern for compositional clarity. Moreover, instead of recording a spontaneous instinctive response to the natural world, *La Danse* presents a complex riddle drawn from the imagination.

Specific interpretations of the imagery based on literary, emblematic and religious readings have proved inconclusive and *La Danse* can perhaps more fruitfully be approached in the context of a long pictorial tradition of dancers and bathers. Derain had already treated this pastoral theme in *L'age d'or* (The Golden Age, 1905; Teheran, Museum of Modern Art), the only painting from his Fauve years to rival *La Danse* in scale. If Derain did indeed conceive of *La Danse* in this tradition, he has thoroughly altered it. Particularly striking is the non-western quality of the image. Derain had visited the collections of the British Museum while in London and had access to similar ethnographic material in Paris. He was certainly also influenced by the Tahitian paintings of Paul Gauguin, which he saw in the collection of Daniel de Montfreid in 1905 and again in the retrospective at the Salon d'Automne in 1906. Around 1906-7 Derain carved a pair of wooden head and footboards for Ambroise Vollard which resemble Gauguin's woodcarving and are remarkably close in imagery to *La Danse*. However, *La Danse* is more obviously otherworldly than Gauguin's work. It has a mythic primordial quality which, in its grandeur of expression, reflects Derain's changing artistic ambitions.

5

MAURICE DE VLAMINCK (1876-1958)
Nu Couché, 1905
(Reclining Nude)

Provenance

Ambroise Vollard, Paris; Etienne Bignou, Paris; Galerie Beyeler, Basel; Private collection.

Maurice de Vlaminck received a modest artistic training far removed from the formal instruction of the École des Beaux-Arts and for him painting would always remain primarily a matter of instinctive self-expression. Like his father, the young Vlaminck gave violin lessons to support himself. He did not seriously consider a career as a painter until he met André Derain in 1900. The two artists started working together in Chatou that year and in 1901 Derain introduced his friend to Henri Matisse at the van Gogh exhibition at Galerie Bernheim-Jeune. Vlaminck was powerfully moved by this retrospective and his work would remain substantially indebted to van Gogh, both technically and in its intuitive relationship with nature. Vlaminck exhibited five paintings at the 1905 Salon d'Automne. In 1906 the dealer Ambroise Vollard purchased the contents of his studio, securing his immediate future as a painter. He was given his first solo exhibition by Vollard in March of the following year. With Henri Matisse and André Derain, Maurice de Vlaminck formed the creative core of the Fauve group.

Although Vlaminck was principally a landscape painter, a small group of nudes survives from his Fauve period. It has been suggested that this example depicts the artist's wife Suzanne. The artificiality and direct nature of its eroticism is perhaps closer in spirit to contemporary depictions of the Parisian *demi-monde* of prostitutes and dancehall entertainers. The reclining nude model is shown looking out of the painting at the viewer while touching her breast in an apparent gesture of sexual invitation. Her face has been depersonalised; the features loosely sketched in over a white base, with touches of red and green adding to the mask-like effect. The drapery which covers her below the waist is suggested by a few strokes of thickly applied paint, sweeping outwards from the centre. Her body, painted in rich and carefully applied flesh tones, is set off against a shifting background of green, blue, yellow and red. Vlaminck has introduced large dots and strokes into these colour fields from adjacent areas, further heightening the artificiality of the scene and enhancing the overall decorative effect.

6

MAURICE DE VLAMINCK (1876-1958)

Bords de la Seine à Carrières-sur-Seine, 1906
(Banks of the Seine at Carrières-sur-Seine)

Provenance
Ambroise Vollard, Paris; M. Rottenbourg, Paris; Stephanie Faniel, Paris;
Private collection.

After Maurice de Vlaminck and André Derain met in 1900 they set up a studio together in a disused restaurant on the Île de Chatou in the suburbs of Paris. Both artists were local to the area; Vlaminck had lived in Chatou since 1892 and Derain was born there. The two friends painted together in 1900-1 and again in 1904-5, forming what is sometimes referred to as the School of Chatou. Vlaminck certainly took note of the brilliantly coloured paintings that Derain and Matisse produced at Collioure in the summer of 1905 but he had already made considerable progress towards a fully-fledged Fauve style which would rival that of his colleagues in its expressive brushwork and colour. Vlaminck later recalled, "I transposed into an orchestration of pure colours all the feelings of which I was conscious" (Rewald 1953, p. 9). Matisse reacted strongly to Vlaminck's use of pure colours when he visited Chatou early in 1905, "I was unsettled, I was not able to sleep that night" (Freeman 1990, p. 66). It seems likely that Vlaminck's work emboldened Matisse to further pursue his own experimental path.

Vlaminck was deeply attached to the riverside suburbs of Paris. Unlike the other Fauves, who often travelled and painted together, particularly in the summer months, Vlaminck professed to have all that he required along the suburban banks of the River Seine. Carrières-sur-Seine was a small town upstream from Chatou. Vlaminck described it as favourite painting spot where the hills gave a view of the whole Seine valley. This view, however, is taken from the riverbanks. The composition has been divided into bands of electric colour with the pink and red strip in the foreground possibly indicating a footpath. The two trees interrupt the horizontal composition, the colour of their trunks passing arbitrarily from red and orange to green and black. The web of branches, painted in loose single strokes of saturated red, contrasts dramatically with the sky and river. The transformation of this conventional unassuming scene into a spectacle of blazing colours is a powerful testimony to Vlaminck's vision and the inspirational effect of his native landscape.

7

ALBERT MARQUET (1875-1947)

La Passerelle à Sainte-Adresse, 1906
(The Pier at Sainte-Adresse)

Provenance

Dr. A.M. Boulard, Créteil; Galerie Schmit, Paris; Private collection.

Albert Marquet trained in the studio of the Gustave Moreau at the École des Beaux-Arts together with Henri Matisse, Henri Manguin and Charles Camoin. He was particularly close to Matisse, whom he had first met at the École des Arts Décoratifs and with whom he would later attend the art classes run by Eugène Carrière at the Académie Camillo. The two artists frequently painted together in these years and were engaged in closely related investigations of colour. As was the case with the other Moreau alumni Marquet showed work at the Salon d'Automne and the Salon des Indépendants and exhibited in group shows at Berthe Weill's gallery. He signed a contract with the dealer Eugène Druet (who was also his chess partner) in 1905. Marquet was deeply impressed by the paintings which Derain and Matisse produced at Collioure in 1905, describing them as "stunning" in a letter to Manguin (Freeman 1990, p. 79). The bold use of colour and expressive freedom of the Collioure paintings inspired a period of experimentation in Marquet's work but he generally favoured a more naturalistic mode and employed a relatively restrained palette.

Sainte-Adresse was a resort town on the coast of Normandy near Le Havre, popular with both artists and tourists. Marquet painted the pier on several occasions during the summer of 1906, when he was working in Normandy with Raoul Dufy. This is one of the most experimental views. Marquet has largely ignored the colourful beach tents and parasols and the elegant clothes of the tourists, which were traditional points of interest in such scenes, in favour of a powerful *contre-jour* effect which transforms the strollers on the pier into dense black shapes. The hot late-afternoon sun is rendered in rings of white, yellow and purple, its radiating strength further suggested by the strong directional strokes of blue in the sky. The depiction of the pier, which seems to shift in angle between the right and left sides of the painting, adds to the unsettling and slightly hallucinatory effect. The rapid brushstrokes and the large areas of exposed paper suggest that this work was painted with considerable speed, almost certainly in the open-air.

8

HENRI MANGUIN (1874-1949)
La Sieste [Jeanne couchée sous les arbres], 1905
(The Rest, or Jeanne reclining under trees)

Provenance
Mme E. Druet, Paris; J. de Rohozinski, Paris; Henri Manguin, Paris;
Pierre et Lucille Manguin, Paris; Private collection, Paris; Private collection.

Henri Manguin trained in the studio of Gustave Moreau at the École des Beaux-Arts in Paris, forming particularly close friendships with fellow students Henri Matisse and Albert Marquet. Manguin's trip to visit Matisse in Saint-Tropez in the summer of 1904 initiated a life-long attachment to the Midi region. He returned with his family the following summer, renting the Villa Demière in Malleribes. The landscape around the Villa Demière provided the setting for a series of idyllic pictures featuring Jeanne Manguin, the artist's wife and favourite model. One of these, also entitled La Sieste and showing Jeanne resting outside, was included in the Salon d'Automne of 1905. Manguin clearly valued the conditions around the Villa Demière. Writing to Matisse from Cavalière, between Saint-Tropez and Toulon, in May 1906, he complained of the heat and the lack of privacy for his models, adding "I miss the Villa Demière and its nice shade" (Freeman 1990, p. 90).

Manguin's depiction of his wife lying in the shade of a tree is intimate and carefree; a contribution to the idyllic image of the sun-drenched south. Jeanne is shown leaning on a cushion with her head supported in her right hand. Her hips are tilted up slightly, creating a long curving line which tapers off to her crossed feet. The colours are generally naturalistic, with the sunlight dappling Jeanne's body and falling in golden tones around the central area of purple-blue shade. The overall effect is restrained and classical, and invites comparison with Renaissance prototypes. There is little evidence of the challenging modernity of Édouard Manet's celebrated *Olympia* (1863; Paris, Musée d'Orsay) or of the Symbolist ambiguities which characterise Paul Gauguin Tahitian nudes.

9

CHARLES CAMOIN (1879-1965)
Port de Marseille, c. 1904-1906
(Port of Marseilles)

Provenance
Galerie Laurenceau, Paris; Private collection.

Charles Camoin met Albert Marquet, Henri Matisse and Henri Manguin in the studio of Gustave Moreau at the École des Beaux Arts in Paris. He exhibited successfully with his colleagues in group shows at Galerie Berthe Weill and also showed work in the two modern Salons, including five paintings at the Salon d'Automne of 1905. However, of all the painters of the core group it was perhaps Camoin who was least comfortable with the Fauve label and that which it implied. He was particularly uneasy with the expressive emotional characteristics of some Fauve painting, preferring instead to pursue a broadly descriptive practice.

Camoin met Paul Cézanne in 1900, while on military service in Arles, and the two artists continued to correspond until Cézanne's death in 1906. There is little evidence in Camoin's work of an attempt to assimilate Cézanne's style but the friendship may have strengthened his artistic convictions. Camoin remained a staunch defender of the importance of painting directly from nature and resisted using colour in an aggressively non-naturalistic manner. Although he also painted a notable group of nudes, the bulk of his work during the Fauve years consists of landscapes, often painted during travels with Manguin and Marquet in the south of France. This sensitively observed view of Camoin's home town of Marseilles is rendered in a relatively cool palette of whites and blues, enlivened by strokes of red and purple. The fort on the hill across the harbour, bracketed by the masts of the two central ships, provides a clear focal point for the composition. Camoin's pleasing and relatively conservative paintings were commercially successful. Reporting in April 1905 on an exhibition at her gallery which featured the Gustave Moreau alumni, Berthe Weill stated "It is Camoin who is leading at the moment in terms of sales, with Marquet in second place" (Freeman 1990, p. 68).

OTHON FRIESZ (1879-1949)
Paysage à La Ciotat, 1907
(Landscape at La Ciotat)

Provenance
Mme Verbois, Paris; Private collection.

Like Georges Braque and Raoul Dufy, Othon Friesz came from Le Havre in Normandy. Both he and Dufy studied locally with Charles Lhulier at the École Municipale des Beaux-Arts and subsequently attended classes in the studio of Léon Bonnat at the École des Beaux-Arts in Paris. At this time Friesz was painting in a loosely defined Impressionist style characterised by a muted tonal palette. Friesz was the only one of the Le Havre Fauves to show at the 1905 Salon d'Automne, however, his work was not installed in the controversial Fauve room 7. Seeing the boldly coloured paintings of Henri Matisse and his colleagues encouraged Friesz to pursue more experimental path. "Colour", he would later say, "appeared as our saviour" (Freeman 1995, p. 24). Friesz was one of the founders of the Cercle de l'Art Moderne in Le Havre, an organisation which in late May and June 1906 presented the first exhibition to include all the core Fauve artists.

Othon Friesz spent the summer of 1906 with Georges Braque in Antwerp, and Braque again accompanied him to La Ciotat on the Mediterranean coast near Marseilles in May 1907. Friesz had already turned away from the bruised pastel shades of his Antwerp pictures in favour of richer colours and a more linear treatment of form. He further extended these stylistic developments in the countryside around La Ciotat, creating a series of experimental and highly original Fauve works. In this example Friesz has typically left large areas of the canvas unpainted. The contours of the mountains and the main features of the surrounding landscape are loosely drawn in with the brush, with shorter chopping strokes adding weight and colour to selected areas. Most of the colour has been concentrated in the middle ground where several houses can be made out tucked among the trees and hills. The curvilinear organic quality of the image is characteristic of Friesz's work at La Ciotat and represents a distinctive contribution to Fauve painting.

RAOUL DUFY (1877-1953)
Les Passants, c.1906-7
(The Passersby)

Provenance
Anonymous sale, Paris (30 April 1931, lot 23); Private collection.

Raoul Dufy was born in Le Havre and initially studied at the École Municipale des Beaux-Arts under Charles Lhullier. He met Othon Friesz in 1893 and, after winning a local scholarship, joined Friesz in Léon Bonnat's studio at the École des Beaux-Arts in Paris. Like Friesz, Dufy initially worked in an Impressionist style, influenced in both technique and choice of subject matter by the strong local tradition of *plein air* painting in his native Normandy. However, the experience of seeing Henri Matisse's Neo-Impressionist *Luxe, calme et volupté* at the Salon des Indépendants in 1905 had a profound effect on him: "...impressionist realism lost all its charm for me as I looked at this miracle of creative imagination at work in colour and line" (Freeman 1995, p. 127).

Dufy developed substantially during his Fauve years. The views of towns and beaches which he painted along the coast of Normandy in the summer of 1906 are characterised by pastel tones of orange, purple and green. This work is more obviously experimental. The composition is framed by two trees which create a stage-like setting for an informal scene in a seaside park. Exceptionally large areas of the primed white canvas have been left exposed. The emptiness of the central area is particularly daring and serves to disperse the viewer's attention around the semi-circle of figures. In the background two strollers are shown with arms raised to their hats, perhaps in greeting or possibly against the wind coming off the sea. In fact, the calligraphic simplicity of the figures resists such close anecdotal interpretation. Composed as flat shapes of one or two colours, they can almost be read as musical notations, with the intervals of blank canvas giving the composition an unusual rythmic quality. The dog in the lower right-hand corner recalls designs by Pierre Bonnard, and the general decorative effect is perhaps closer to an Art Nouveau sensibility than it is to Fauvism.

12

RAOUL DUFY (1877-1953)
Les Barques aux Martigues, 1907
(The Boats at Martigues)

Provenance
Galerie Bernheim-Jeune, Paris; Fridart Foundation.

This is one of three versions of *Les Barques aux Martigues* which Raoul Dufy painted in the autumn of 1907. It represents an important moment in Dufy's stylistic development and also illustrates the tension which had newly entered Fauve painting. Fauvism's liberated use of colour has here been joined by an interest in the structural treatment of form.

Martigues is a coastal town north-west of Marseilles. In this view the yellow shoreline acts as a band at the top of the composition, tilting it forward and compressing the pictorial space. The perspective shifts throughout the painting; even the individual boats in the foreground appear to have been painted from different angles. Dufy has represented the boats in a highly schematic way, reducing them to angular quasi-geometric shapes. The structural quality of the space and the overall sense of density is heightened by the treatment of the water, where reflections and shadows blur with equally powerful but unrelated passages of parallel brushwork. Several of these features are attributable to the growing influence of Paul Cézanne whose structural and volumetric treatment of form was also affecting other members of the Fauve group at this time. Dufy adjusted the colours and arrangement of the boats in each of the three surviving versions of this composition. He would soon abandon Fauvism altogether in favour of a form of Cubism.

13

GEORGES BRAQUE (1882-1963)

Port de L'Estaque, 1906

(Port of L'Estaque)

Provenance

Jacques Dubourg, Paris; Private collection, Paris; Alex Reid & Lefevre, London;
Private collection.

Georges Braque was born in the suburbs of Paris but grew up in Le Havre where his father worked as a house painter. He returned to Paris in 1900 and joined the Académie Julian. Following the completion of his military service in October 1902 he enrolled in the Académie Humbert and also studied briefly in the studio of Léon Bonnat at the École des Beaux-Arts with fellow *Havrais* painters Othon Friesz and Raoul Dufy. He probably met Henri Matisse and André Derain at the opening of the Salon des Indépendants in March 1906.

Braque was the youngest of the Fauves and did not exhibit at the 1905 Salon d'Automne. His early Fauve style emerged in the summer of 1906, while painting in Antwerp with Othon Friesz. By the end of the year the two artists were in L'Estaque, a small coastal town near Marseilles where Cézanne had also worked. Painting along the shore and in the hills around L'Estaque, Braque created a distinguished group of high-Fauve works characterised by the confident liberated treatment of colour. The colour scheme in this example is particularly vivid. The side of the boat pulled up on the shore near the viewer is composed of a daring combination of yellow, pink and red with touches of green and lilac. The organic forms of the beach are also typical of Braque's work at L'Estaque. When André Derain visited the town towards the end of 1906 he reported to Maurice de Vlaminck that "Friesz, Braque are very happy. Their idea [about painting] is youthful and seems new to them" (Freeman 1990, p. 97). Braque would indeed later characterise his Fauve period as a passing youthful preoccupation; an imperfect step in his emancipation from the demands of conventional representation.

Braque returned to L'Estaque several times in 1907 and 1908. In the summer of 1908 he began a series of landscapes there which not only rejected Fauve colour but also challenged the foundations of Fauve painting as an intuitive and spontaneous practice. Several of these works were included in an exhibition at Galerie Kahnweiler in Paris in November 1908. In his review Louis Vauxcelles, the originator of the term 'Fauves', noted that Braque was "reducing everything, site and figures and houses, to some geometric schemes, to cubes" (Freeman 1990, p. 113).

14

KEES VAN DONGEN (1877-1968)
Torse (L'Idole), 1905
(Torso, or The Idol)

Provenance

Georges Grammont, Paris; Charles-August Girard; Mme Pomaret, Aix-en-Provence;
Ellen Kyriazi, London; Fridart Foundation.

Kees van Dongen was born in Delfshaven near the Dutch port of Rotterdam. He spent a year in Paris from July 1897 and moved to the city permanently in 1899. Van Dongen initially worked as an illustrator, as he had done in Rotterdam, but he also developed a powerfully expressive form of Neo-Impressionist painting. He gravitated towards Fauvism in 1904/5 but was never a close member of the core Fauve group. His association with the Fauves is based principally on his affinity for strong saturated colours, vigorous brushwork and use of dark outlines.

Van Dongen's wife Guus was the model for this extraordinarily bold and sensual work, which was first exhibited at the 1905 Salon d'Automne. Although it was not displayed in the controversial 'Fauve' room 7 of the Salon, it rivals the work of the nascent Fauves as the expression of a forceful and original creative personality. Guus is shown nude with her arms behind her head, eyes closed and face turned to one side. Her pale body, sculpted in heavy black and brown lines, is set off dramatically against the shifting dark background. Guus's face has been painted in distinct bands of colour, with white on lower jaw passing through three deepening shades of pink to brown across her forehead and nose. These colours communicate Guus's emotional state and heighten the intimate aspect of the image.

Van Dongen met Max Pechstein of the *Die Brücke* group in Paris in 1907/8 and later exhibited successfully with the German Expressionists. After the First World War he concentrated increasingly on society portraits.

15

KEES VAN DONGEN (1877-1968)

Le Hussard (Liverpool Light House), c.1907

(The Hussard, or Liverpool Light House)

Provenance

Pierre M. Bloch, Paris; Commandant Cormouls, Paris;

Palais Galliera, Paris (12 March 1964, lot 36); Marlborough Fine Art, London;

Private collection.

Unlike the core group of Fauves, Kees van Dongen was not principally a landscape painter. He is most closely associated with the nightlife of Paris's Montmartre and Pigalle districts, where he painted the *demi-monde* of dancehalls and entertainers in the spirit of Toulouse-Lautrec and the young Picasso. He excelled at capturing the energy and slightly intoxicating or hypnotic quality of establishments such as the Moulin de la Galette and the Rat Mort.

This composition, which was first exhibited at the 1908 Salon d'Automne, is based on a lost drawing and a painting which van Dongen made around 1897-8. A hussar, identifiable by his uniform, is shown outside the Liverpool Light House, a dancehall in the Dutch port of Rotterdam. A second couple can be made out approaching an indistinct blur of lights and colours at the lower left. In the related drawing the two women standing in the doorway at the right are nude. The Liverpool Light House was almost certainly also a brothel and we may speculate that both these two women and the hussar's partner are prostitutes. The pose of the hussar, with his arched legs and thrusting hips, certainly seems to suggest a sexual encounter. Van Dongen had already made a series of watercolours of Rotterdam's red light district for the *Rotterdamsch Nieuwsblad* and also produced the illustrations for a special issue of the French satirical journal *L'Assiette au beurre* on the life of prostitutes in 1901.

16

LOUIS VALTAT (1869-1952)
Le Taxi [Boulevard à Paris], c.1905
(The Taxi, or Paris Boulevard)

Provenance
Monsieur Blache, Versailles; Private collection.

Louis Valtat's inclusion in discussions of Fauve painting is partly due to a critical review of the 1905 Salon d'Automne in the publication *L'Illustration* where his work was reproduced together with that of Henri Matisse, Henri Manguin and André Derain. In fact, Valtat's work was not exhibited with that of the Fauves in room 7 of the Salon and is only peripherally related to Fauvism in its strict historical sense. Valtat may be more usefully studied in the general context of the increasing importance of colour in French painting around 1900. The works which he produced in 1895-6 in Arcachon in south-west France show a liberated use of colour which is often described as 'proto-Fauve'.

This lively sketch records a typical Parisian street scene with two figures resting on a bench near a car. Some of the patches of colour can be interpreted as awnings or shop fronts, with the evenly spaced dark blocks at the top edge possibly indicating windows. The speed of execution gives the work an appealingly spontaneous quality and suggests that it was painted directly from life. The arbitrary cutting of details such as the figure at the lower edge and what may be a second automobile in the lower right-hand corner, enhances the sense of a short-hand notation done on the spot. The manner in which Valtat has captured the car, the single tree and the figures with a few simple strokes of the brush invites comparison with Raoul Dufy's similarly calligraphic technique in *The Passersby*. Like Dufy, Valtat has also left parts of the primed canvas unpainted.

RECOMMENDED READING

Duthuit, Georges. *The Fauvist Painters*. Trans. Ralph Mannheim. New York: Wittenborn, Schultz, 1950.

Rewald, John. *Les fauves*. Exh. cat., New York: The Museum of Modern Art, 1952.

Derain, André. *Lettres à Vlaminck*. Paris: Flammarion, 1955.

Elderfield, John. *The 'Wild Beasts'. Fauvism and its Affinities*. Exh. cat., New York: Museum of Modern Art, 1976.

Oppler, Ellen Charlotte. *Fauvism Reexamined*. New York & London: Garland Publishing, 1976.

Giry, Marcel. *Fauvism: origins and development*. Trans. Helga Harrison. New York: Alpine Fine Arts, 1981.

Freeman, Judi. *The Fauve Landscape*. Exh. cat., Los Angeles: Los Angeles County Museum of Art, 1990.

Whitfield, Sarah. *Fauvism*. London: Thames and Hudson, 1991.

Flam, Jack. *Matisse on Art*. Berkeley & Los Angeles: University of California Press, 1995.

Freeman, Judi. *Fauves*. Exh. cat., Sydney: The Art Gallery of New South Wales, 1995.

Le fauvisme ou "L'épreuve du feu". Exh. cat., Paris: Musée d'Art Moderne de la Ville de Paris, 1999-2000.

EXHIBITION CHECKLIST

Measurements are in centimetres, height before width.

Georges Braque (1882-1963)

Le Bateau Blanc, Anvers, 1906
(The White Boat, Antwerp)
Oil on canvas
38.5 x 46.5

Port de L'Estaque, 1906
(Port of L'Estaque)
Oil on canvas
50 x 61

Les Bateaux à L'Estaque, 1906
(Boats at L'Estaque)
Oil on canvas
46 x 55

Charles Camoin (1879-1965)

Port de Marseille, c. 1904-6
(Port of Marseilles)
Oil on canvas
73 x 93

André Derain (1880-1954)

Pêcheurs à Collioure, 1905
(Fishermen at Collioure)
Oil on canvas. 46 x 54

Le Cheval Blanc, c.1905-6
(The White Horse)
Oil on canvas. 46 x 38

La Tamise et Tower Bridge, 1906
(The Thames and Tower Bridge)
Oil on canvas. 66.5 x 99

La Danse, c.1906
(The Dance)
Oil and distemper on canvas
185 x 228.5

Kees van Dongen (1877-1968)

Le Violoncelliste du Moulin de
la Galette, 1905
(The Violincellist of the Moulin
de la Galette)
Oil on canvas. 65 x 53.5

Torse, 1905 (Torso)
Oil on canvas. 92 x 81

Le Hussard (Liverpool Light House),
c.1907
(The Hussard, or Liverpool Light House)
Oil on canvas. 101.2 x 82

Raoul Dufy (1877-1953)

Le 14 Juillet au Havre, 1905
(July 14 at Le Havre)
Oil on canvas
46.5 x 38

Vieilles maisons sur le bassin d'Honfleur,
1906
(Old houses along the Honfleur dock)
Oil on canvas
60 x 73

Trouville, 1906-7
Oil on canvas
54 x 65

Les Passants, c.1906-7
(The Passersby)
Oil on canvas
46 x 55

Les Barques aux Martigues, 1907
(The Boats at Martigues)
Oil on canvas
54 x 65

Othon Friesz (1879-1949)

Paysage à La Ciotat, 1907
(Landscape at La Ciotat)
Oil on canvas
33 x 41

La Ciotat, 1907
Oil on canvas
65 x 80

Paysage fauve aux arbres, 1907
(Fauve landscape with trees)
Oil on canvas
32 x 40.5

Henri Manguin (1874-1949)

La Sieste (Jeanne couchée sous les
arbres), 1905
(The Rest, or Jeanne reclining
under the trees)
Oil on canvas
50 x 61

Albert Marquet (1875-1947)

La Passerelle à Sainte-Adresse, 1906
(The Pier at Sainte-Adresse)
Oil on paper mounted on canvas
50 x 61

Henri Matisse (1869-1954)

La Plage Rouge, 1905
(The Red Beach)
Oil on canvas
33 x 40.6

Femme au Kimono, c.1906
(Woman in a kimono)
Oil on canvas
31.5 x 39.5

Les Voiliers, 1906
(The Sailboats)
Oil on board
25 x 59

Nature morte aux fruits et fleurs, 1906
(Still life with fruit and flowers)
Oil on board
32.4 x 60.4

Louis Valtat (1869-1952)

Le Taxi (Boulevard à Paris), c.1905
(The Taxi, or Paris Boulevard)
Oil on canvas
22.5 x 24.3

Maurice de Vlaminck (1876-1958)

Nu Couché, 1905
(Reclining Nude)
Oil on canvas
27 x 41

Nature morte, 1905
(Still life)
Oil on canvas
53 x 72

Bords de la Seine à Carrières-sur-Seine,
1906
(Banks of the Seine at Carrières-
sur-Seine)
Oil on canvas
54 x 65

Bateaux à voile, c.1907-8
(Sailboats)
Oil on canvas
73 x 92